KINGFISHER
READERS

level
3

W9-AWG-537

Creepy–
Crawlies

Anita Ganeri
and Thea Feldman

KINGFISHER
NEW YORK

KINGFISHER
LONDON & NEW YORK

Series editor: Thea Feldman
Literacy consultant: Ellie Costa, Bank Street College, New York

ISBN: 978-0-7534-7090-9 (HB)
ISBN: 978-0-7534-7091-6 (PB)

Kingfisher books are available for special promotions and
premiums. For details contact: Special Markets Department,
Macmillan, 175 Fifth Ave., New York, NY 10010.

For more information, please visit
www.kingfisherbooks.com

Printed in China
9 8 7 6 5 4 3 2 1
1TR/0713/WKT/UG/105MA

Picture credits
The Publisher would like to thank the following for permission to reproduce their material.
Every care has been taken to trace copyright holders. However, if there have been
unintentional omissions or failure to trace copyright holders, we apologize and will,
if informed, endeavor to make corrections in any future edition.
Top = t; Bottom = b; Center = c; Left = l; Right = r
Cover Shutterstock/Vaclav Volrab; Pages 6t Shutterstock/Danyichenko Iaroslav;
6b Naturepl/Philippe Clement; 7 Frank Lane Picture Agency(FLPA)/Paul Hobson;
8 Shutterstock/Daniel Prudeck; 9 Shutterstock/teekaygee; 10bl Science Photo Library/
Dr. John Brackenbury; 10bc Shutterstock/Peter Waters; 11t Ardea/John Clegg; 11b Ardea/
Steve Hopkin; 12 Shutterstock/VasilyVishnevskiy; 14 Shutterstock/orionmystery@flickr;
15t FLPA/Treat Davidson; 15b Shutterstock/Cathy Keifer; 16 Shutterstock/Alexey Filatov;
17t Shutterstock/2happy; 17b Shutterstock/Evgeniy Ayupov; 20 Naturepl/Kim Taylor; 21t
Naturepl/Nick Upton; 21b Shutterstock/orionmystery@flickr; 23 Naturepl/Hans Christoph
Kappel; 24 Shutterstock/Cathy Keifer; 25t Naturepl/Stephen Dalton; 25b Naturepl/Kim
Taylor; 26 FLPA/Thomas Marent/Minden; 27t Ardea/Ian Beames; 27b Shutterstock/Platsee;
28 FLPA/Pete Oxford/Minden.

Contents

Meet the creepy-crawlies!

What are creepy-crawlies? Some of them are **insects**. That includes ants, butterflies, and earwigs. Spiders are creepy-crawlies too. And so are snails and slugs. Earthworms and **millipedes** are also creepy-crawlies.

What makes them creepy-crawlies? They are all very small animals!

Ladybug

Beetle

Slug

Snail

Look at all the creepy-crawlies below. Are you ready to meet a lot more?

Butterfly

Spider

Millipede

Grasshopper

Bee

Ladybug

Worm

Ants

Beetle

Earwigs

5

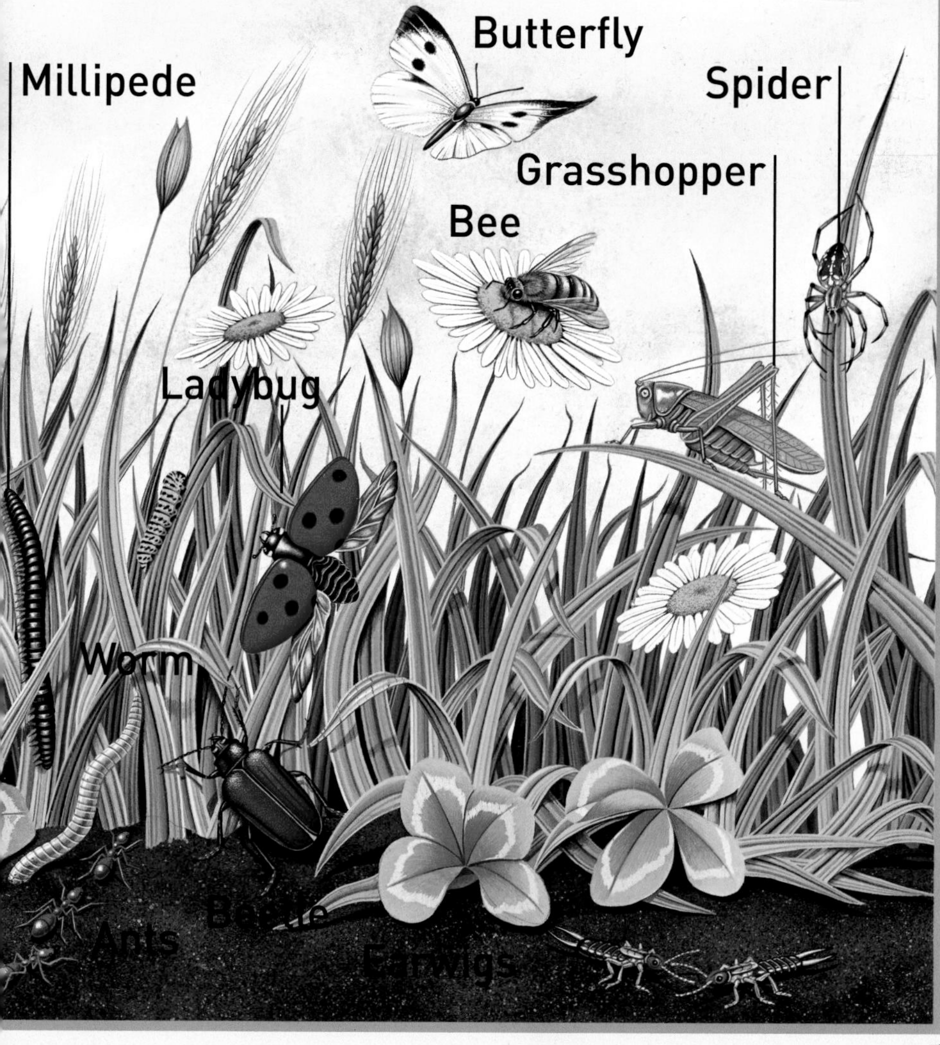

They are everywhere!

It is easy to find creepy-crawlies outdoors. Butterflies feed on flowers. Spiders spin webs on fences. Ants march through the grass. Creepy-crawlies live in gardens, parks, fields, and woods. They are almost everywhere on land!

Did you know?
Earthworms are creepy-crawlies that live underground.

A lot of creepy-crawlies live near or in
bodies of water. That includes ponds, rivers,
and the sea. Some kinds of spiders, snails,
and beetles live under the water. In the
photo above, a dragonfly perches near a
pond. It is looking for other insects to eat.

Legs to count on

Insects are the most common creepy-crawlies. Here's an easy way to tell if a creepy-crawly is an insect. Count its legs! An insect has six legs. If the creepy-crawly has more legs (or less legs), it is not an insect.

Eye

A honeybee is an insect.

Antennae

Wings

Legs

Count the number of legs on the spider below. The spider has eight legs. That means it is not an insect. Spiders are **arachnids**. All arachnids have eight legs.

Legs

Fang

Eye

Did you know?
Millipedes have a lot more legs than insects or spiders. Some millipedes have 375 pairs of legs—that is 750 legs!

On the move!

Some creep. Some crawl. Others fly, hop, or **slither**. Creepy-crawlies move in many different ways.

A grasshopper jumps using its long back legs. It jumps to get away from hungry birds. The grasshopper leaps high in the air. It opens its wings and flies away.

Did you know?
A honeybee flaps its wings about 250 times a second to stay up in the air.

A water boatman is an insect that lives in ponds. It lies on its back like a boat in the water. This bug uses its back legs like oars to row itself forward. It looks for **tadpoles** and small fish to eat.

Did you know?
Snails leave slimy trails behind them. They make slime to help them slide across the ground.

11

Traveling near and far

Many creepy-crawlies creep and crawl close to home. A few make very long journeys. Every year thousands of monarch butterflies travel roundtrip from North America to Mexico. They spend the winter in Mexico where it is warm. They travel up to 3,000 miles (4,828 kilometers) one way! The globe-skimmer dragonfly goes almost twice that far. It flies roundtrip from India to Africa every year.

Did you know?
Some birds follow the dragonflies as they fly—and eat them!

Did you know? Some monarch butterflies fly to the same trees in Mexico every year!

Creepy-crawly senses

Creepy-crawlies use their senses to find out about the world around them. A fly has two huge eyes on the sides of its head. Each eye has thousands of tiny **lenses**. These allow a fly to see very well.

Did you know?
A cricket has ears on its front legs near the "knees." They are tiny holes with skin stretched across the top.

Insects use **antennae** on their heads. This male moth has antennae that look like feathers! An insect's antennae can sense smells and also taste and touch things.

Did you know?
Spiders cannot see very well. They use hairs on their bodies to help them feel their way around.

Creepy-crawly meals

Different creepy-crawlies eat different things. Many eat leaves, stems, and flowers. A bee visits a flower to drink **nectar** and eat **pollen**. Some pollen falls onto the bee's body. Some of that pollen will fall off the bee when it visits the next flower. New flowers grow when flowers share pollen. Bees do not know it, but they are nature's tiny gardeners! Some bees bring back pollen to their nest for other bees to eat.

Creepy-crawlies eat different things. A
leech is a kind of worm that drinks the blood
of other animals! And some creepy-crawlies,
like the mantis below, eat other creepy-
crawlies! This mantis is eating a spider.

A butterfly's life story

1

2

3

4

Some creepy-crawlies change a lot as they grow up. Here is how a tiny egg becomes a beautiful butterfly.

1. In the spring, a female butterfly lays eggs on a leaf.

2. The eggs hatch. A caterpillar wriggles out of each one.

3. The caterpillars eat the leaves. They grow much bigger.

Did you know?
A female butterfly can lay 100 eggs every day!

5

6

7

4. Each caterpillar makes a hard case. It is
a safe place to stay. It is called a **chrysalis**.

5. Inside the case, the caterpillar turns into
a butterfly.

6. The chrysalis splits open. A butterfly
comes out! Its wings are soft
and wet.

7. The wings dry
in the sun. The
butterfly flies
away.

Some caring mothers

Most creepy-crawlies lay eggs. Most
leave the eggs to hatch by themselves.
An earwig takes care of her eggs. She
stays by the nest. She cleans the eggs
with her mouth. Once the eggs hatch,
the earwig watches over her babies.

A female wolf spider lays dozens of eggs. She makes silk and wraps it around herself and the eggs. The eggs ride on her belly until they hatch. Then the babies move to her back. They stay there for a few weeks.

Creepy-crawly builders

Some creepy-crawlies build nests. Honeybees build a nest together. A honeybee nest is called a **hive**. Honeybees make beeswax with their bodies. They use it to build tiny little rooms inside the hive. Some rooms hold eggs. Other rooms hold honey.

Some creepy-crawlies build traps to catch food. A trapdoor spider builds a **burrow** under the ground with a door. The spider waits inside by the door. It senses when an insect comes along. It opens the door, jumps out, and gets a meal!

Did you know?
Termites are tiny insects that build big, tall nests called termite towers. Some can be about 30 feet (9 meters) high!

Biting and fighting

Spiders catch and eat other creepy-crawlies. Most spiders have two fangs they use to bite and kill prey. Poison travels through the fangs and goes into the prey. The creepy-crawly dies and the spider eats it.

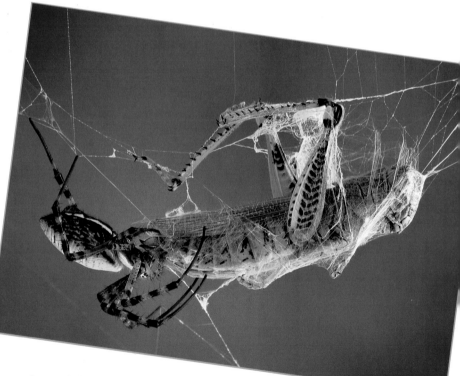

A spider kills prey trapped in its web.

Many creepy-
crawlies are prey
for other animals.
Some creepy-
crawlies fight
back! A wasp uses
poison when it
senses danger. It
shoots poison into
an enemy through
a stinger in its
tail.

Hiding in plain sight

Can you see the insect in the photo below? The mantis is the same color as the flower. That makes it hard for other insects to see it. It is a creepy-crawly that uses its colors to hide from prey. When another insect lands on the flower, it attacks!

Did you know?
A hawk moth has
spots on its wings.
To a hungry bird,
they look like
big, scary eyes.

Some creepy-crawlies use their colors
to keep from being eaten. The leaf
insect below is green and also shaped
like a leaf. It blends in with real leaves
and stays safe from hungry animals.

A huge creepy-crawly!

Spiders are creepy-crawlies. Most creepy-crawlies are small animals. But some spiders are not small. This hairy bird-eater is huge! It can be as big as a dinner plate.

This spider crawls out of its burrow at night to look for food. It eats insects, other spiders, lizards, and even small birds! It grabs prey with its long legs and bites with its fangs. It is one big, tough spider!

Did you know?
A bird-eater spider hisses if it is in danger. Then it flicks hair at an attacker's face.

Glossary

antennae long, thin parts of an insect's head that are used for smelling, tasting, and touching things

arachnids creepy-crawlies with eight legs. Spiders are a kind of arachnid

burrow a hole a creepy-crawly digs in the ground to live in or lay its eggs in

chrysalis the hard case that a caterpillar makes around its body

hive a nest built by bees

insects creepy-crawlies with six legs

lenses the part of the eye that focuses the light coming into the eye in order to help an animal see things clearly

lizard a type of reptile. Other reptiles include snakes, crocodiles, and tortoises. All reptiles have scaly skin

millipedes creepy-crawlies with many pairs of legs. Some millipedes can have up to 750 legs in total

nectar a sweet liquid inside flowers that many insects drink

pollen something powdery in flowers that bees and other insects eat and is also needed for new flowers to grow

slither to move along by sliding

tadpoles baby frogs or toads

Index